difficult news

difficult news

poems

valerie berry

Sixteen Rivers Press • San Francisco

The following poems first appeared in these publications:

Genesis, "cadaver lab"
VIVO, "looking there"
Western Journal of Medicine, 1988; 149(6). "intensive care"
Used by permission of BMJ Publishing Group.

O

The first line in "Rumi's question" is from quatrain
number 747 in *Open Secret: Versions of Rumi,* translated
by John Moyne and Coleman Barks (Threshold Books,
1984).

The epigraph that introduces "bird in hand" is from
Hummingbirds: Their Life and Behavior, by Robert Tyrell
and Esther Quesada Tyrell (Crown Publishers, Inc., 1985).
Used by permission of Crown Publishers, Inc.

The italicized lines in "tonight I can write" were
inspired by a poem in *Twenty Love Poems and a Song of
Despair,* written by Pablo Neruda, translated by W. S.
Merwin (Chronicle Books, 1993).

O

Published by Sixteen Rivers Press
P. O. Box 640663
San Francisco, CA 94164-0663

O

Library of Congress Catalog Card Number: 2001-131036

ISBN 0-9707370-0-9

for those who have gone to hell for love

i. *directions*

directions   3
night vision   5
hitting the wall   8
cadaver lab   9
walking man: Rodin   10
the fallen caryatids: Rodin   11
for Nancy Roeske   12
two women at a small-town
    foreign film festival   13
intensive care   15
finding the way home   20

ii. *dead man in a Greek restaurant*   21

iii. *winter's north coast*

Mendocino   31
the father on the bridge   45

iv. *saying the name*

raking leaves   51
difficult news   53
blackbirds at St. Patrick's seminary   55
the soft day   56
untitled   57
looking there   58
deciding to buy the blue vase   59
first lesson   60
Rumi's question   61
bird in hand   62
on violets and nonviolets   63
crossing the ecliptic   64
tonight I can write   65
year end gift, California   66
April's fool   67

i. directions

directions

There is a way of opening a walnut
so that the kernel plops in your hand
like a small, perfect brain,

and two ways of slicing an apple
so that you see a heart or a star
that no one else has ever seen,
and, if the knife is quick and sharp,
white pearls inside the brown husks of seeds.

There is a way of slicing an onion—
the squat red kind—that reveals arches
within arches, a labyrinth leading
to the pungent center of the earth.

There is a way of measuring a tree
that tilts time on its edge,

and a way of looking into the sky
so that you see the inside
of your own eye.

There is a way of speaking to a child
that opens a secret door
and treasure pours out.

There is a way of looking at a woman
that turns her into someone
you have never seen,

and a way of looking at a man that
turns him into someone you
have never seen.

There is a way of opening yourself
that feels like death—because it is—
with no hint of its ultimate surprise:
afterward you stand up, pulling your flesh
about you like new clothes.

There is a way of losing your mind
that is like waking from a feverish nap,

and a way of sitting in silence
so that what you love most
is drawn to your side,

and you have known all this
since before you were born.

One day, if you are lucky, someone
will look at you, turning you into
someone you have never been—
aware, suddenly, of informing marks
in the dust at your feet, your pockets
full of maps showing the way to
the next thing, intriguing clouds leading
beyond the edge of the world.

night vision

1

Sometimes the bottom drops
out of your brain and the anguish
you've kept bundled inside

shows its face, staring back
from whatever direction
you choose to look, catching

at your sleeve if you try
to outrun it. Sometimes it comes
in bright sunlight—more often

on a late hour, a long hour,
maybe one you spend driving in dark
between cities bent backward by

the horizon, two distant pools of light
separated by a valley filled with fog.
Passing fields flicker at the edge

of your vision like streams of faint stars,
light so dim they're seen by *not* looking,
extinguished by all but the most sideways glance.

Acres of unpicked cotton grow monstrous
in the mist until you're lost in tule fog,
the pavement going nowhere past

the reach of your headlights, white clot
erasing direction and destination, erasing
even the hour that holds you.

2

The fog is dense as angel cake,
wide as the ancient sea that once filled
this valley—but not deep.

As if anchored by your night vision,
a bright kite of stars, the Pleiades,
rises above the fog bank's east rim,

the tug of their distant mass—important
if unmeasurable—reaching for you across
light's long journey.

Those seven sisters climb heavenward
like celestial bees, cluster like friends
in warm bars on nights of foul weather,

sharing tables filled with empty glasses,
air thick with the scent of October fog
dripping from wool sweaters, and yes, light—

if you dare let it leak into your
broken places—white light constellated
in sideways smiles, each

steady candle, each glance.

3

Tule fog and absent sea,
and whatever rises out of them
to make the hour worth the cost.

Headlights glow in approach,
and for a moment your beams weave
in the fog, a brief handshake,

both hello and good-bye.

And when the white wall billows up,
any direction can be the one
you choose, leaning toward

that distant gravity of *home*
stretched on the horizon, all roads
leading deeper into the night.

hitting the wall

In April I am off-season,
        growing older as the greening comes.
            I run after the rain,

each step loud with breath
        and slap of rubber sole
            on wet pavement.

I curse the Second Law
        of Thermodynamics—the one that says
            in time, everything falls apart.

Defying age, momentum and mass,
        I lean too far at the next corner and
            go down, air punched from my lungs.

Between heartbeats it's all some damp,
        anaerobic dream—I forget how
            to breathe, drown in April haze.

While synapses sputter and spark,
        time slows, until I have a whole
            lifetime to cherish the scent

of bruised grass,
        lilac, cement
            wet with spring rain.

cadaver lab

We keep each in a humidor like
fine, forbidden Cuban cigars, rare
harvest for select students, or so says
a sign on the outer door.

You know, of course, that we name them,
name them for what they became: artless,
empty husks, willed to us. We unband,
unroll and personify; each name
a summation and anthem.

Stained coats and stainless steel,
intensity by rows. We study silence—
and science—the aromatic air: phenol,
not ash of rose.

If only we could graft back the art,
and watch "Mister Peabody"—when
his liver lived—play taproom darts,
guzzle in foam, or seduce a cigar
with a match. But we can't;
we probe, but no one's there.

(A hand in surgeon's glove
spans this lesser Sistine
and brushes empty air.)

walking man: Rodin

Something gnawed this man,
took off his head, his arms, left
the rest standing in mid-stride.
His torso hangs in rips and chunks,
imperfect nakedness torn by
hunger so big that raw inertia
is all that's left. Faceless, hand-
less, turned away, the hole where
his right kidney should be
is mouth enough.

    Below the wound
that was his genitals, thighs curve
in perfect agreement, take weight
without quivering. Knees lock
in firm extension, a gesture signing
to bend is to be weak. Farthest from
the pain, his toes grip the step he
won't complete, fused by the work
of denying what kills him—bronzed
moment of another man, walking.

the fallen caryatids: Rodin

Close to Orpheus, their backs
to the Gates of Hell, they balance
their burdens in a slow,
bronze falling.

Supple as trees these women
fold into themselves, assuming
the unborn shape left long ago
for the difficult work
of their straightening.

Now weight breaks the symmetry
of shoulders in
graceful collapse.

One carries water; one
bears a stone. Each holds
a hand to steady the thing
that crushes her.

Each turns her face away from that hand.

On the planes of their cheeks
light lies smeared like fine oil,
lips press against wrists
as if tasting the gleam—

what flesh knows of its
own endurance, shining
like a blade.

for Nancy Roeske

One day, after lunch, that year
before you died when no one knew
you would, we talked about what kills
women doctors. We discussed the literature,
facts crisp on our tongues, our four hands dumb
among sandwich plates and teacups, the bread knife
relaxed on the cutting board.

Those kitchen academics proved all *Abstract*
and no *Conclusion*. What keeps coming back
is just this summary of gesture: your hand on edge
scraping crumbs into a whole-wheat pyramid,
the tiny pile flattened by one moist fingertip,
the crumbs carried slowly to your mouth,
your hand undulant, awkward—a next-to-
last gesture I saw, but did not see—your hand
lifting like a bird at the start of
long flight, before it finds
the rhythm of distance.

two women at a small-town foreign film festival

We enter, daring to be hip, taking in
the latest thing in celluloid, the old Vogue
warm, red velveted and dark. We enter,
glad for anonymity, the scent of popcorn
reminding us of backyard coops where hens
scratch the dust, hiding eggs and hurtling
into hedges when the chicken hawk
comes. We enter, night-blind, stumbling,
find two seats together and settle down
like birds waiting out an eclipse of the sun.

The film rolls: some sweet old story
of lovers and a lust that cuts across cliché
because I've never seen women kiss
like that, the brunette hovering over
the blonde, arched in a gentle feathering
that is both familiar and far away.
Something clicks inside my head
and I'm up in the balcony, looking down,
a bird's-eye view of the audience
perched in neat rows. I see myself,
hawk-heavy brow, Birkenstocks over
wool socks, and a head taller than
my "date": a bird-boned woman tied
to earth by her tiny Italian shoes.
All color goes in the low light. Black
and white, we flicker in the strobe
of this same old scene.

I think then of the flesh that's passed
beneath my hands, all the women

who've offered themselves for my close
diagnostic look. I flex those hands, full of
the feel of breasts and bone and the warm
red darknesses I've touched . . . and then
it happens: above the subtitles a woman's lips
move in language I suddenly understand.
To her question,

> *How are you different*
> *from us two lovers*
> *tangled in the light?*

I whisper,

> *The same.*

Final scene. A train leaves the station
and the lover with most to lose
leaps on board into waiting arms.
A final kiss. The End. Lights come up.
Color washes over us, couples stand,
stretch, move uphill together away
from the nest of shabby seats—but
my bird-boned friend claws at my wrist.
Her eyes have captured the black light,
blanked out, eclipsed by some shadow seen
too sudden and too close. I think if I
leaned into her, put my ear to her breast,
I would find a heart ripped open, some
inner division blown out like a veil
in the wind, hear the murmur of blood
seeking new paths, a heart ready for
the demand of wild wings released,
beating their way into the light.

intensive care

1

Dorothy smells sweet in her dying.
Her infection, pseudomonas, consumes her
like a crumbling stick of honey incense.

Sparked from rough coals of cancer dug
from her belly, the smoldering spreads,
burns in sheltered corners in her lungs.

We force air into her through a hole
in her neck: another surgery, another
wound that will not heal.

We forget a simple rule:
Don't chase cancer
with a knife.

2

Dorothy, I never knew you whole.
Comatose from the first day, you have lain
these weeks with eyes turned in on

who can tell? Pain,
or memory, or the bright
glow of your dying?

Maybe the sweet combustion
of bacterial growth is a scent that
centers you in that old, deep brain.

If I knuckled your chest where the bones
show thin, you would only flex
your wrists in a limp salute,

or your jaw would quiver open-close,
open-close, the way wild animals grimace
for the taste of prey.

3

Your men are gone.
Father, husband, sons who waltzed with you
have faded into wallpaper roses.

There is no one to lead you in this last
number. We are two girls in white, left
to learn the final steps together.

It always comes down to this:

women teaching women how to live.
Dorothy, my grandmother, my child,
I feel too young for this mothering.

Gloves off, I take your hands,
burning with the infectious fire
beating in your blood,

hot sparks pumped round and
around by the tired iamb
of your heart.

4

Late afternoon; we'll pretend there's time
for tea and little biscuits and crumbs that fall
to the pink napkin in your lap.

Flowers bloom in corners sheltered from
the swish of passing dancers, musicians
are blowing notes under the swaying palms,

feel the beat, Dorothy, one-two,
one-two, like wild animals
pacing in a cage.

A sweetheart waits in the knife-edged
shadows of those potted palms,
and when the music stops—

when the music stops—
he will ask you for
the next dance.

5

The air folds into you
like layers of perfumed
tissue paper.

Here is a red rose
to burn in the ash
of your hair.

I tell you, Dorothy,
it is time
the music stopped.

finding the way home

As if you could not learn
to unwant it: the illusion
that walls stay, strong and standing,
the roof tight against rain.

As if what you bring into the house
is more real for your choosing: a white vase
with ragged lips, the green-bellied
kerosene lamp, new knives.

As if what you pull into
the center is not also and always
edge.

As if the hearth in the corner could be
the contraction of fire, and not just
one more place you save embers
at the end of day.

As if not gift enough
those coals, ash wrapped,
enduring,

       as if not themselves the embodied
       longing of every ring of stone raised
       above a flat, grassy plain.

ii. dead man in a Greek restaurant

1

He is quiet and polite, no one noticing he's turned the blue of a man not breathing. He'd settled his bill, left an adequate tip on the table before slipping away, slumping across two café chairs on his trip to the door, near an old woman with small eyes, pulling on a cigarette between bites of pita bread, her table next to mine where I sit counting my dissatisfactions: baklava with more pistachios than I prefer and too little honey, wishing the woman would take her cigarette outside, her eyes crazy enough that I know better than to call a waiter and make a scene.

2

someonemygodcallanambulancejesushelp

3

No one expects a dead man to show up between bites of baklava—the kind of thing guaranteed to change the direction of your day, if not your life. I'm ashamed to say that later I'll try to make a poem of it, telling myself that he is *my* dead man, my stiffening muse. I'll lean on the memory of his dusky face as if on a sharpened stick, try to make the words flow. I'll take him walking over hills wet with late rain, float his blue face high up into a shredded eucalyptus, where a raven will perch, croaking, and I'll watch myself take ownership of *it*, glad as hell it showed up in the poem, the first lines forming:

> *there has always been a raven*
> *waiting for the day I walk*
> *a dead man up the hill*

But it won't work, and I'll know it, feeling desperate and stupid as the poem starts to fail, but then the raven will tilt its head like a lover begging to be kissed, and I'll clutch at that image, at the chance to write a different poem—one beginning *the raven tilts its head like a lover begging to be kissed*—leaving the dead man up a tree while I scout around for what might shine next to a black bird I've just declared the embodiment of love, pausing to see what I can make of cursive slug slime at my feet, the cracked-heart hoof marks of deer, the scented, disrobing trees. I'll discover—even though he's here only in my imagination and refusing to fit into my poem—that a dead man in a Greek restaurant is a hard thing to not write about.

4

Because I could do something, I had to do something. Later, I'll remember the brown stains on his teeth, the orange sauce in his beard, the line of sun freckles below the collar I unzipped, looking for a tag saying he just might want, or not, to stay dead. I'll remember the piss stains on his trousers—sure sign of something dying inside—the tickle of mustache against my lip, how hard it was to tilt his head on his fat neck, the pounding we gave him. Someone helped me but I won't remember her name, distracted by the arrival of something that wasn't there, the dead man going and something coming, something with a pink, mobile face—peaceful, dazed at the fuss—saying his name was Frank, that all he needed was a glass of water, really, just a glass of water.

5

Out of this, poems I cannot write—and shouldn't—
words that fail as only words can fail, their imperfection
a reminder that life is more than what crafted phrase I
can make of one dead man in a Greek restaurant, felled
on a spring day among my silent bitchings about ciga-
rette smoke and the quantity of nuts in a dry baklava. He
said I saved his life—searching words, meant in grati-
tude, and something else, something he looked for in my
face, an unasked question I don't know how to answer,
unless to say, *This is not a question. It was Friday, Frank, too
many pistachios but good coffee, an old woman with crazy eyes
gnawing on pita bread, a raven I hadn't yet met, late rain yet
to fall, one more glass of water, a gesture in each moment that
is all there is—your good luck, maybe, that there was some-
thing I could do, and my better luck, maybe, that your dying
and return were just in time, and just enough, to remind me of
the uses and limits of words.*

iv. winter's north coast

Mendocino

1

Fern Canyon, so deep the weather
seldom changes—this wooded cleft
carved by clouds wrung out as they
climb the Coast Range just inland,
and what roars in from the sea skips
over the high loft of sequoia and fir,
hard rain broken by canopy until
what falls, finally, at bottom, is mist.
The sky is green and the ground is
green, and second-growth trees rise
a long way before branching—
each one ridged, in right light, with
greeny phosphorescence.
Whatever lives here has learned to
live slow, acquainted with determined
missions of moss, the patient
fingering of ferns.

2

I came here in winter because it was where
the momentum of my life had brought me.
I came with nothing that I could not
live without, and even that was too much
to keep on carrying. I came empty, but
not hungry—a failed marriage the least
of what ailed me—and I came alone,
in that way you can be alone only
once in your life if—after staring down
the hell of it—you choose
to go on living.

3

A long way off the path, I found a stump
lying open and red, its punk pulled apart
as if ripped by lightning—but no, not in
that deep place, and no hole sizzling
in the high green sky. Next to my boot,
the telltale scrape where it slipped—
the clawed paw of whatever came after
whatever comes after a rotten stump,
my gasped word for it hanging white
in cold air: *bear*.

        To a nose that can
sniff out the sweetness of grubs, I
reeked of blood, my body keeping its
old contract with the moon. To whatever
charts her hunger map stump by stump
I was garnish, savory perhaps, something
tasty at the edge of her plate. If I were
to be torn it was too late for fear,
and the long, airless moment listening
for the crash of ferns taught me that
not breathing changed nothing,
except to make me dizzy.

4

Some nights, on the steep side
of Albion Ridge, dogs ran loose
in the woods, the echoes with nowhere
to go but out over the river, unrelieved
by moon. The Milky Way rose above the trees
on the opposite shore—a plume of cold and
distant smoke—the pitch of dog voices
drawing the shape of what
they bayed: a lone deer.

Those nights I lay awake and imagined
that knotholes in the cabin were peering
down at me, imagined what ran across
the river, how the howling stopped: a hot
throat torn, jaws reddened with
vicious satisfaction—until, one night,
I heard a splash, and the frenzied
disappointment of dogs told me
that the doe was swimming for
my side of the river,
and making it.

5

Along the Mendocino coast the headlands
fall away to a rocky strip of beach—the drop,
one that would kill me, if I wanted. And in those
wrecked days when I had nothing else—not even
hate—to weigh me down, I wanted, floating
over fields marked *No Trespassing,* not caring
if the owner set his dogs on me or let fly
with birdshot, drawn to the edge as if I were
a compass needle that had lost its lodestone,
or star, and could point now only to water,
deep, deep water.

6

The Greeks have a saying: *Do not sleep*
beneath a cypress, because if you do
you will be changed when you wake.
Some days, deep water calling,
the tree break was as far as I dared,
the wind off the sea sighing in dark,
contorted limbs. It was a winter
of too little rain, the grass lying long
and flat and dry, and what sun there was
struggled through salt haze: weak, warm
only in low or sheltered places—the lee
of trees or wedged among rocks. I slept.

7
Sometimes even a small dream
is big enough: I saw a black fern
fall, twisting from high in the sky,
saw it arrow in and stand erect among
brittle hands of last year's bracken . . .
and I woke, wounded, as if pierced
by the thing, wondering if this was how
the earth was clothed—the garden simply
dropped on us—and if what we got from
the angels, what turned us human, was
nothing more than the notion of loss.

Something crossed the sun.
A shadow hovered, looking down:
not angel—at least, not one I knew—
this one knobby-headed, black,
circling what had come to lie so still
in a barren field, a long tooth missing
in the grin of its left wing.

8

In late afternoon the salt fog rolls in
at a rate a woman walking just fails
to outpace, a cold eclipse that spreads
itself up tall cliffs, toxic to what has not
been bred to bed in it.

           I let it have my back,
hands busy with the jaw in my pocket,
a bone I'd found sleeping among
cypresses, bone of some long-absent
thing that drew dark birds to circle
the memory of carrion, found
by my simple act of lying down on it.
And I, alive enough to wonder what
it was that bit my shoulder, discovering
a stone snarl with something of a lion
about it—and dog—like some fierce
guardian of hushed Asian temples,
its teeth blunted by years
gnawing wind and sun.

9

Seal, he said, *a young one. Dogs*
or crows or something must have
dragged it up from the beach after
it was dead—long time ago. There's
been nothing in that field since before
I can remember, except maybe
some lambs—some folks like it
that their flesh picks up the salt—
but not lately. The wild dogs
won't leave them be.

10

Across Albion Valley you can see where
lightning has walked: dead snags at
the tips of trees, some with scars and
a ladder of scorched limbs running
down one side to the ground; but those
that have not been struck stand pliant,
green. In late winter, before dog violets
flare in ditches, ospreys take aim
at the trees, hauling dry limbs to restore
their nests loosened by storms. Once
I saw a bird dive hard at the bare arm
of a Douglas fir, saw the limb tear away
and start to cripple, before the *crack!*
of its breaking caught up with me—
it was that far, and that clear, and
that still.

11

I worked hard to stay warm—staying warm
meant I stayed alive—and chopping wood
is what it took. I learned what burned hot:
oak, if you could find it, madrone, if you
had the patience, and redwood, if the pile
was as big as a house and you fed the stove
hour after hour. I learned what burned
without heat: fox fire eating rotting stuff
under the trees; the cold light of glowworms
awakened by my fire and signalling like
slow trains along the logging road where,
more than once, I stepped out to look up
(because nothing closes in like
a small cabin on a winter night);
and, of course, stars.

12

I wish I could say that I came to
a better understanding of myself,
but there is a reason why ancient people
of the earth carved spirals into rock:
reminder that we know only where we
start, and whatever comes, circle out in
wide experience, that central dot a centering,
something we constantly leave behind and
return to, until we die.

13

Two things I don't know how to place,
even now, long out of the woods, what I
keep returning to. First, that January day
before I learned to aim an ax, flailing
at the woodpile and wet with sweat:
I heard every branch and twig along
the Albion start to hiss, saw the blue wall
of a winter squall roar up the valley, saw
a torrent of pearls driven by the wind—
hail, like every dispassionate eye of
the earth—cold, cataracted,
glancing off whatever stood
in its path. I dropped the ax, tore off
my clothes, and let the hard sting of ice
do what it would, my body white,
then pink, then steaming.

The other: Fern Canyon, that day
I held my breath after breathing *bear*.
Nothing happened, a nothing of
such nothingness that I turned
full around, feeling cheated, as if
my suffering needed to be a thing
with teeth, something separate, wild,
with a hunger that I claimed to
own no part of. I turned, and in
that turning, saw where I had come:
to a ring of trees risen from roots
of a bear-blasted stump, something
sawn down and dead a full century
past, yet nourishing still
with its slow decay.

> And I knew that, if I were to
> go on living, I would accept
> this consolation: that it was
> worth all my invented heavens—
> the hope of fine children and
> bright weather—to stand,
> however broken, at the center
> of my life and know it.

the father on the bridge

1

Cruising high above Russian Gulch,
    on the mesh of bridge where
        the highway narrows,

I see you walking, stranger, tall
    as a father should be, your
        nylon jacket wind-broken back,

you uncaring in cabled wool,
    your face brushed crimson
        by the rising Mendocino wind.

You are smiling, or maybe just breathing
    through your mouth, a happy gap
        between your front teeth,

I'll bet you could whistle up anything,
    you have chosen to be this unafraid,
        this free,

your buccaneer's mustache the color
    of your boy's hair, the son hanging on to
        the meat hook of your hand,

his fine, wild hair fluttering
    like a half-grown gull
        hovering for a handout . . .

and I want to stop right there on the bridge,
    block oncoming traffic until snarled
        logging trucks and hippie vans

make it safe to run beyond their barricade,
    run, the dangerous traffic now stopped
        and still, I want to run

and hang myself on
    to your other,
        empty hand.

2

Sometimes this is how a poem comes, lightning seeking ground, these bolts from the blandest blue. It doesn't matter where or what or whether I'm up to it, it simply takes me, dangerous sometimes, sometimes like this, hanging out over Russian Gulch, car in gear, back seat full of folded laundry and groceries, a dozen eggs balanced delicately on a loaf of whole-wheat bread, the checkbook unbalanced, me thinking of anything but the thing that is coming, the thing that overwhelms—like a door that opens in the middle of a cartoon sky and a shocked Elmer Fudd looks out and down—you can see all of poetry on his face—amazed at finding himself someplace he never knew existed. That's the moment, the joy of beholding, before fear and Newtonian physics and remembering what's impossible takes over, and he scrambles back into the sky and slams the door. This is dangerous. I think someone should know about it, these fits of poetry, these trap doors and land mines. Make it a standard question at the Department of Motor Vehicles, right up there with *Do you wear glasses? Have you ever had seizures or loss of consciousness? Have you ever been stricken by a poem?*

3

Many famous poets refuse to tell you
what their poems mean, as if there were
rules to this affliction, some reliable
ars poetica. Good enough reason for
me to tell you this: It's about more
than fathers and bridges. It's about
longing for someone or something I'd
wreck several lives for, if it meant my own
would be saved, if it meant being
hand held across that bridge—full feathered,
white winged, and soaring when I got to
the other side. It's about longing for
someone or something that would hang on
to my heart with hands like hooks,
until the time came to let me go, until
the time came when I could let go,
my spirit free and whistling through
that happy gap, unafraid, and
becoming anything.

iv. saying the name

<u>raking leaves</u>

Already a long, lingering fall.
Cracks in the earth reach toward
each other in a garden I've
stopped watering, the tomato vines
gone brittle and leafless, the last of
the Sweet 100's lying red and wrinkled
in the dust. I should double-dig, put in
a cover crop of vetch or fava beans,
coax nitrogen back into the beds.
But the only task I care about is
raking leaves, falling now in waves
of yellow and saffron, perfectly
dry, smelling of long-empty
bottles of perfume.

> The leaf heap rises, its small pyramid
> transforming the backyard into something
> I welcome, these days, when loss is
> too much on my mind, knowing I'm
> not ready for the rain, and the long
> grey before green.

> In another life, I knew how to
> crawl under leaves and listen for
> the turning, knew how to let it
> take me, years ago. Death was somehow
> cleaner then, when pyramids preserved
> mystery, when what died was still royal,
> lovely beyond rot: the queen recumbent in

her cloak of hammered gold, her smile
one that comes from knowing a word
for this other than *November.*

Falling leaves tick as they settle on a lawn
I've just raked clean. The tree that sheds them
stands half empty, the sky promising
more days like this one: dry, blue, still.
The springy metal tines say *sing! sing!*
as they scratch the hard earth. I lean
on the rake, the sun low and warm on
my face, and listen for anything
I can say in answer.

difficult news

There is a woman hidden
in this picture. Look for something
about to move: strain in the rock,

a hard knee bent in
incalculably long prayer.
Look for the intention of slow roots,

her foot levered against
the simple machine of her heel.
The rock folds and shelves in

familiar patterns: wedge of coiled shadow,
arched vault of belly—a geometry
invisible by day. You must learn to

see in the dark, see through stone,
trust the body's inclination—your salt
pulled by the collapsed star of her hand.

See the face you cannot see,
her head turned away, left ear pressed
to the mumble of pebbles. Her lips are

moving in darkness, suckling shapes
of forgotten vowels. Wait.
Soon, you will hear them.

See her smooth breast breaking free of
fractured chert. See her shoulder gleaming,
emeried by the sun's rough kiss.

The dust is turning to bone, to skin,
to touch; your mouth fills, remembering
the taste of living things dug from the earth.

The air between you shrinks into
shared breath, the ache of your ribs
unhinged by the hollowness of hers.

She is about to lift her hips from the lock
of deep time, to shine from some
hidden center. What you have never lost

can come back to you, streaming through
this window-stone, this woman-rock-shining,
woman of eyes turned away, turning to gaze

into eyes that are ready to see. *Come.*
It is only the hardness of possibility.
Look for something about to move.

blackbirds at St. Patrick's seminary

In this light, don't call them black.
Say another name, more precise
for the precision of their beaks: fine tools
at work in the feathers' yellow foil.

They come every evening, face west
on wires I wish we had strung from
our imagining the glitter that burns
in these dark birds.

Our faith seems a dull thing, the sound
of bells swung at dusk, saying *night
is coming, night is coming.* On this
cold confidence, the birds turn
their backs, take light as they
find it—groomed, gathered,
gold—their cracked calls
the perfection of song.

the soft day

What *can* fall is down and ordinary;
what won't stay buried, shines.
Last week frost killed what the drought
left, water lines burst in white hemorrhage,
loss that mocked my summer measured in
cupfuls of grey water.
                    But today is
a soft day; my hands appear from
my pockets, leave their fists behind.
Another long swing around the sun
begins, and I know there are no
level places, just this uncertain center
within changes of change and
change, changing.

Under a dying hedge a hermit thrush
is looking for his song. He coughs
the clenched, unpracticed notes, all
he knows so far of January, the sky
dappled by blackening leaves—his song
of praise for leggy, edible, reminding
things, easy in the velvet soil stretched by
the hard freeze, unaccountably alive
in the softness of shattering.

untitled

Two years now, and finally I sleep
in the middle of the bed, dreams
tucked in around me. Sometimes you
are there—not kind the way I know
you can be kind, but that other way,
the cold man who lives inside you and
will not warm himself or look out of
your eyes, unafraid of what it is
to be a man: not cold, not unkind, not
hiding in dreams.
                 I turn in bed, crying out,
know you are both those men, and more.

Sometimes the morning sun makes
strange shapes of light and shadow
where the curtain eases in the wind.
Once I woke and knew you were
beside me, at the edge of touch—
innocent, whole—for as long as I
could lie there and not turn to
make sure. And once, not long after,
spilling through the lace, the sun lay
a smooth, warm hand across the bed
and, in language it is taking my
lifetime to understand, wrote
                 memory
                      memory
on the rough, white wall.

looking there

First day of February in a
bad winter—the California kind,
a cold somewhere not quite wool-deep,
and damp to the bone, but no rain, still,
no rain. What weighs on me is all mine.
Clouds climb over the Santa Cruz hump
and graze overhead, grey bellies full of
what I think I yearn for. But I am wrong.
What comes over those hills, out of that sky,
is just this: clouds not yet ready to rain.
I turn my face like a flower seeking
different light, splinter of some
better prism, and find it *there*, glowing
in a fallen thistle, skeletal leaves spread
like a lace fan. And *there*, shining along
the bald, speckled skull of a Japanese man
bent down to prune suckers from the base
of his apricot trees. And *there, there,*
there—radiant in three of last year's
fruit, shriveled back to the hard pit,
but clinging, still, to branches too high
to reach, not yet ready to fall, each one
full of only what it needs to be filled with.

deciding to buy the blue vase

takes two days of searching my house
for some opening in air where
a blue vase the size of a small child
can stand. Two days, thinking,

> I have never owned
> a blue vase the size of
> a small child,

and finding it takes time, remembering blue:
the eyes of a man I once woke up next to,
remembering, too, why now I don't,

or those blue-marbled postcards from
Istanbul another man kept sending,
saying, *like this, just like this —*

time for my longings to settle
where I want them. I'm lucky;
I could have waited much longer for

this blue vase, raku glazed,
lifted whole from the white-hot bed
of burnt pine needles where so many

shatter—no one knows why—but for me,
only two days and it's mine, a thin
drift of pine ash clinging still
inside its blue, oval lip.

first lesson

In April we walk—you ask me
the names of things. I say *bay
laurel, Umbellularia californica,
also known as pepperwood.* But
nothing happens until I crack
the spine of a slender leaf, hold it
to your nose. Suddenly, your face
is full of tree light, saying the
name, over and over.

Rumi's question

Is the one I love everywhere?

Answer *yes.*
There are times when to be right is
to be right out of your head.
Imagine one thing that covers all,
like a blanket—it's what you want on
cool summer nights. You could say *stars,*
for all we know of them: a sameness
made infinite.

Answer *no,*
and you invite a stranger to enter.
There is bread on the plate, a cup
for wine, a cat circling the table,
looking up for something that might
fall off the edge. Fall off the edge and see
what pounces. Break yourself into pieces
and see who comes to look in your face.
Go with him, even if he doesn't ask
your name before picking your pockets.

bird in hand

*In some parts of Mexico the body of
this little bird is considered a potent
love amulet, and that just holding
it in one's pocket will draw the
object of love's desire.*

Lured by the promise of red,
a hummingbird flirts
with my glass jar
of sweet water.

He floats in a globe
of sound, low vibration
beating in my ears at
bones fine as his.

He flaunts a slow flex of torso
blurred by staccato wings and,
needle-quick, sews my eye
to all his edges.

In my garden, bright lips
of fuchsia open for
his kiss and he

dances away, supple body
squeezed in green sequins,
iridescent, alive.

Migrant pulse in perfumed light,
heat stored against the night—
I would keep him in *my* pocket
for more than luck.

on violets and nonviolets

after Hopkins

I rage for more violets, dark
nightdrifts of blossom, the passion
of failed saints come spadeshaped
and lovely, dark frenzy of violets,
force up from winterunder, sweet
underfoot splitted by leaf armies
of longing.

Nonviolets don't move me; give me
essence empurpled, hordes marching
sunhungry, March sprung from below.
A disciplined earth throws seed with
abandon and violets by fistfuls fill
full up the dead fields, fill far deep
the dark ends, dull wood lots defeat.
I rage for them—rage!—with blooddeep
desiring for violets darkcoming,
coming, coming.

crossing the ecliptic

Because we are busy with lives
we think are ours, we miss the
middle places, impressed only
by extremes: the shortest day or
longest night. The earth tilts; we
hold on, the slow slide of light
something that slips by unnoticed.
Look up. Each day the day is changing.
Listen: slow, dull gold, light's ringing
like a fading bell. By latitudes we prepare
for sleep or waking. The sun's no longer
biting here, while half a world away
it grows a smile. Which lingers longest?
Spring, sap rising, every sexed thing
grown wild with wanting? Or this,
the cooling night we pull around
our shoulders? Spring, for all its fire,
completes in fall. What blossoms, breeds,
sets seed, burns out. Full of fruit the trees
are going back into their bones,
each leaf a loss, with long nights ahead
to count them. What lets go goes deep
and we follow, gladly, perhaps for
well-earned rest, or to practice death,
or for nothing more than our dark joy
of riding earth through another turning.

tonight I can write

after Neruda

the most joyous lines, write "For love,
all the waterfalls are flowing up to the sky!"
Ducks swim upside-down, broad orange feet
paddling the air, the water running with
coppery slicks leaked from their feathers.

Tonight, the insides of things are revealed.
I breathe the air of astonishment. Long ago,
another poet wrote of joy flowing through
unmarked boxes, and look! Here it is, again.

Tonight I find it, as plain cardboard boxes
dissolve into light, amber-red vapor roaring
through pipes and flutes. Work of the sun,
pocketed by trees, tonight spills out
in a thousand, thousand places.

For joy the sparks fly out. For joy the earth turns
into something we can breathe, great chunks
of mountains whistling through our lungs.

What does it matter that we don't stay small
inside ourselves? That the mountains, for joy,
turn hollow and take us inside?

What does it matter that we keep forgetting this?
Tonight, I remember what is possible: joy come
without footprints, like those upended ducks,
stepping on air.

year end gift, California

Fifteen feet up, braced on a leafless branch,
he says, *Gotta pick 'em now else the crows'll
get 'em, or them bees —*

       waving his fruit hook
at the cloud hovering over a broken roof tile,
sluggish in the December cold.

       Here you go . . .
and he tosses one down, hard as a baseball,
but pointed—the tree laden, its amber fruit
catching the sun like fat, old-fashioned
Christmas lights.

       *Gotta wait for 'em to ripen,
a week or two on the window sill. One
might be ready for Christmas, but for sure,
come the New Year, you'll be eating 'em
with a spoon, sweet as pudding. You
look me up if I'm not telling the truth.*

April's fool

for Nathan

Pruning water sprouts from the
elderly plum, I turn to greet you
as you walk up the drive, saying—
as you often do of that fifteen minutes
when the evening turns luminous—*Look,
it's the magic hour*. And, loving the joy
in your face, I forget about the blades,
close them on the tip of my longest finger,
hear the piece of fingernail flick among
dried leaves, feel the news of stunned flesh
before pain, before blood, and, still
savoring your smile, I close my thumb
into the wound like a clumsy Buddha
tricked into performing this mudra,
replying, *Yes, it is lovely, isn't it?*

Originally from Indiana, Valerie Berry is a physician living in the San Francisco Bay Area, writing and reinventing her practice of medicine. She misses Indiana tomatoes and thunderstorms, and is consoled by hummingbirds and San Francisco fog.

Sixteen Rivers Press is a shared-work, not-for-profit poetry collective dedicated to providing an alternative publishing avenue for San Francisco Bay Area poets. Founded in 1999 by seven women writers, the press is named for the sixteen rivers that flow into San Francisco Bay.

16 RIVERS
P·R·E·S·S

SAN JOAQUIN • FRESNO • CHOWCHILLA • MERCED • TUOLUMNE • STANISLAUS
CALAVARAS • BEAR • MOKELUMNE • COSUMNES • AMERICAN • YUBA • FEATHER
SACRAMENTO • NAPA • PETALUMA